Moritz Dittmar

"The Great Gatsby" by Francis Scott Fitzgerald. Autobiographical Traits

GRIN Verlag

Bibliografische Information der Deutschen Nationalbibliothek:

Die Deutsche Bibliothek verzeichnet diese Publikation in der Deutschen National-
bibliografie; detaillierte bibliografische Daten sind im Internet über http://dnb.d-
nb.de/ abrufbar.

Impressum:

Copyright © 2013 GRIN Verlag GmbH
Druck und Bindung: Books on Demand GmbH, Norderstedt Germany
ISBN: 978-3-656-53138-8

Dieses Buch bei GRIN:

http://www.grin.com/de/e-book/231625/the-great-gatsby-by-francis-scott-fitzgerald-
autobiographical-traits

FACHARBEIT

im Leistungskurs Englisch

Autobiographical Traits in „The Great Gatsby" by

Francis Scott Fitzgerald

Verfasser: Moritz Dittmar

Bearbeitungszeit: 10 Wochen

1.Introduction

"The Great Gatsby", written by Francis Scott
Fitzgerald, and published in 1925, is a socio-
critical novel where he tells the story of a self-
made millionaire pursuing his lost love. It was
praised by famous authors and is to be considered
as one of the best American novels.
Understanding "The Great Gatsby" is important
because this novel gives you a perfect view in to
the roaring twenties. Fitzgerald used often,
autobiographical elements in his novels. In my
essay, I try to consider if one knows the novel
better because of knowing something about the
author's life.

1.1 The Author

Francis Scott Fitzgerald (1896-1940) was born in
St. Paul, Minnesota, on 24 September 1896. He
was educated at Newman School and Princeton
University. Due to academic difficulties he left
Princeton and went to the US Army.
He knew the depict world of New York in his
novel „The Great Gatsby" from own conception.
After college in New York and after an
unsuccessful military service he worked there as a
journalist. His novel „This Side of Paradise"
(1920) helped him to be prosperous in his early
years. Before that he had a glamorous life and
became an idol of the jazz-generation and the
„Roaring Twenties". In the mid twenties he

became friends with the writer Ernest Hemingway and published „The Great Gatsby" in 1925. Soon he broke under his fame and the pressure he felt every day. His alcoholism got worse and his wealth shrank incessantly. Eventually he led a life of self-accusation and worked as a writer for a magazine in Hollywood where he died with 44 years of age due to a heart attack.

1.2 Summary

Nick Carraway, the protagonist of the novel „The Great Gatsby", recently moved to the West Egg District of Long Island, a wealthy area. His neighbor is Jay Gatsby, a mysterious man who often held parties on Saturday nights. As the summer progresses, Nick eventually receives an invitation for a Gatsby party. Nick becomes friends with Gatsby and learns that he is in love with Daisy so they started an affair. Nick knew Daisy from his childhood when they almost married but he was too poor back then. Tom, Daisy's husband, is suspicious and tries to prove that Gatsby is not what he seems. Daisy gets really angry but finds out that Gatsby is not a pharmacist but makes his money through bootlegging. Daisy drives home with Tom and accidently hits Myrtle Wilson lethally. Thinking that Gatsby killed her, Mr. Wilson shoots Gatsby in his own house. No one attended Gatsby's funeral but his Dad and Nick.

Tom and Daisy go to Chicago and Nick never sees them again.

2. Autobiographical elements in novels

An autobiographical novel is a form of using information's of the author's life but also elements of fiction. Because it includes parts of fiction it will not fulfill the "autobiographical pact" and that is why one cannot see the novel only as an autobiography but as a novel with autobiographical elements.[1] The parts of the story like names and locations are often changed but still represent the author's life. Most of the events are exaggerated or altered to make it more dramatic or entertaining to read. The biographical topic helps the reader to better understand basic essentials within a work. It also helps the reader to connect different novels by one author. Furthermore it allows the writer to rely and reflect on his or her own experiences. Nonetheless, an autobiographical novel need not always be related to the author's life but often has to be treated as a fictional work. A lot of novels regarding personal, intense topics like war, family conflicts and deaths are written as autobiographical novels.

---

[1] Philippe Lejeune, "Autobiographical Pact," pg. 19

2.1 Fitzgerald's application of autobiographical elements

All great novels are often based on autobiographical fiction because authors write most efficient when they rely on first hand experiences. Especially Francis Scott Fitzgerald used his own feelings, impressions and experiences for his novel and his short stories. In his essay "One Hundred False Starts," published in 1933, he said: "Mostly, we authors must repeat ourselves and that's the truth. We have two or three great and moving experiences in our lives and experiences so great and moving that it doesn't seem at the time that anyone else has been so caught up and pounded and dazzled and astonished and beaten and broken and rescued and illuminated and rewarded and humbled in just that way ever before.

Then we learn our trade, well or less well, and we tell our two or three stories and each time in a new disguise and maybe ten times, maybe a hundred, as long as people will listen."[2]

On the other hand, Fitzgerald's fiction was not just thinly disguised autobiography it was more transformed and transmuted than a complete autobiography. None of his protagonists like Jay Gatsby or Dick Diver can be fully identified with Scott F. Fitzgerald, nevertheless he allocated a lot of emotions and experiences to them. He always

---

[2] *Afternoon of an Author*, ed. Arthur Mizener (New York: Scribners, 1958), p. 132.

emphasized, that his literature contains autobiographical elements and that it had its origins in his feelings: "Taking things hard from Genevra to Joe Mank: That's stamp that goes into my books so that people can read it blind like brail,"[3] or "Whether it's something that happened twenty years ago or only yesterday, I must start out with an emotion, one that's close to me and that I can understand."[4]

He chose a lot of things out of his life like family, friends, life and locations for his literature to recreate them in a fictional way of capable, conveying trueness as he saw them.

His emotions and expressions for his novel „The Great Gatsby" came from his visit with the Fitzgerald clan of Great Neck, Long Island. Fitzgerald met the writer Ring Lardner who might be the model for the mysterious Owl Eyes. The setting for Gatsby's extraordinary parties in West Egg was provided by Great Neck while the Corona Dump of Queens provided the setting of the valley of ashes where Wilson's garage is. The believing in the „American Dream" by Fitzgerald is represented by Gatsby and additionally by a Long Island neighbor of Fitzgerald who was also a bootlegger and always used the expression „old sport" like Jay Gatsby.[5]

---

[3] *The Notebooks of F. Scott Fitzgerald,* ed. Matthew J. Bruccoli (New York and London: Harcou Brace Jovanovich/Bruccoli   Clark, 1978), # 1072.

[4] "One Hundred False Starts," *Afternoon of an Author,* p. 132.

[5] Scrapbook, Princeton; the clipping is reproduced in the *Fitzgerald/Hemingway Annual* (1976),

3. Autobiographical Traits

3.1 Relationship with Zelda / Daisy

In November 1917, Fitzgerald left to join the army
as a second lieutenant. He never served in Europe
but was sent to Alabama, where he met Zelda
Sayre with whom he fell in love with.
Regardless the love Zelda felt, she refused to marry
him until he could support her and take care of her.
In April 1920 Zelda married Fitzgerald and they
became one of the prominent couples of the
'Roaring Twenties', while living a live of social
and financial abandon.[6]
In the early years of their marriage Zelda and Scott
were public figures, particularly in the nightlife of
New York City. He held a wild life with Zelda.
They behaved like Fitzgerald's fictional characters
and that is no coincidence because Francis Scott
Fitzgerald used some of the uninhibited behavior in
his fiction.
They were hosts of great party's and also attended
them. Parties with alcohol, which was illegal
because of the Prohibition era. They lived the full
life, wrecking cars in parks or going out for a
midnight swim in ponds and parks. Zelda was
always by his side and actually cheered him on
when Fitzgerald attacked a bouncer in front of a
New York City nightclub. They got ejected out of
different residents because of their lifestyle but
exactly that helped Fitzgerald to be the most paid

---

[6] The Great Gatsby, Methuen Notes (Study Aids, 1978)

magazine fiction writer of the twenties. The
publicity helped to sell his stories and the public
nearly expected from him that he would write
those stories with associating to his private life. A
lot of people back then knew that Zelda Sayre
inspired but also destroyed Fitzgerald. She
influenced Fitzgerald's work by her behavior and
her qualities. Zelda helped him to his success and
was a major element of his public portray.
Nevertheless, she was an excessive woman and
disturbed Fitzgerald's actual plans of writing
serious novels. She wanted to make the quick
money through Fitzgerald writing and enticed him
away from his writing but to parties.[7]

However, Zelda had schizophrenia, which labored
their relationship but Fitzgerald was still in love
with her. That irrational love is reflected in Jay
Gatsby's feelings towards Daisy. He took care of
her, especially after Zelda suffered a mental
breakdown in 1930. She recovered fast but
suffered another collapsing. At this time Fitzgerald
knew that Zelda would not recover and that she has
to go to a mental institution for the rest of her life.
Daisy and Jay Gatsby had a superficial relationship
in their early years. Gatsby was too desperate to
get over it. On the other side was Daisy, who
moved along with her life and married. After five
years they found each other again. Being on a
deprivation of Daisy, he has created fantasy of her.
Gatsby imagined Daisy as one of the most
beautiful persons in the world. Consequential
Gatsby was very disappointed when he discovered

---

[7] *The Great Gatsby*, Understanding, Dalton Gross & Maryjean Gross (1998)

that his fantasy about Daisy was not true at all. His life was not as great as he thought it was: "There must have been moments even that afternoon when Daisy tumbled short of his dreams – not through her own fault, but because of the colossal vitality of his illusion. It had gone beyond her, beyond everything. He had thrown himself into it with a creative passion, adding to it all the time, decking it out with every bright feather that drifted his way. No amount of fire or freshness can challenge what a man can store up in his ghostly heart."[8]

After comparing those relationships, both Fitzgerald and Gatsby had handicapped alliances with their loved ones. Both of them refused to recognize that Daisy and Zelda had their faults. Furthermore, both of them built up a fantasy with their respective woman but only in their heads. In reality they actually believed that the fantasy was true.

3.2 Desire for success through failure / Alcoholism

Another parallel, which can be drawn between Fitzgerald and Gatsby, is the dream of success or 'the American dream' that is pursued by both. Fitzgerald was never able to live his dreams and achieve the fame he haunted all life but through Jay Gatsby, he lived it out. Both came from common beginnings. Fitzgerald did not let Jay

---

[8] Letter from Fitzgerald, Fitzgerald (97)

10

Gatsby have a lot of wealth in the beginning just to make his situation more truthful. Fitzgerald wrote most of his dreams into the novel.

Another personal parallel is that both had strong opinions about alcohol. While Jay Gatsby is a non-alcoholic because he had to take care of a drunken guy all the time, Fitzgerald was heavy alcoholic throughout his life. He only had tiny control over his drinking habits. He stopped drinking and became abstinent a couple years later but he developed tuberculosis. It was so bad that he had to take strong medicine to find sleep. Fitzgerald was never proud of his alcoholism and he tried to hide the fact that he was addicted. That is the basis why Jay Gatsby is abstinent his whole life.[9]

3.3 Time and Lifestyle

Because Fitzgerald published his book 1925 it is clear that he wrote it during the roaring twenties. The roaring twenties can be divided into growing wealth, new conflicts, and changes in ordinary life and cultural life.

The fundament of the growing wealth was the economic boom in the USA and the building industry expanded. The government created new conflicts by prohibiting the drinking of alcohol. The prohibition era began which led to gang fights and bootlegging. In that time the biggest change in ordinary life was the car. A lot of people moved to suburbs because they were independent with their

---

[9] http://gatsbyprojecttahs.wikispaces.com/Gatsby+connection+to+Fitzgerald

car. Debts were no longer a shame and people bought expensive consumer goods. All that was financed by advertisement. The culture changed as well because people in the cities were more generous and the entertainment industry grew fast: Theater, concerts and movies were affordable for the citizens in cities. Sports became a big part of society.

The roaring twenties were a time of fun and party. Especially women changed society.

Fitzgerald did not invent the term "flappers" but he coined and popularized it.

Flappers were a new generation of young women who had short skirts, short hair, listened to Jazz and who violated the rules of good behavior with self-confidence. They were cheeky and bold, because they smoked, drank liquor and applied make up. Earlier American women could not have imagined living like the flappers did because it was socially unacceptable.[10]

Flappers often shocked the older generations because of flirting with many men, dating widely and allowing them to be kissed.

Besides their disrespectful behavior flappers distinguished oneself through their own fashion. The origins came from the Jazz-era. The short hair became popular and the flappers stopped wearing a bodice because it was uncomfortable to dance with it.

Despite all the scandals through flappers the fashion of being a flapper was forced through and even some older ladies changed their lives.

---

[10] *The Great Gatsby*, Understanding, Dalton Gross & Maryjean Gross (1998)

Notwithstanding its popularity, the lifestyle of flappers did not survive the world economic crisis in 1929. In following time of big economic problems was no space for the love of life and the hedonism the flappers pursued.

4. Is "The Great Gatsby" an autobiography?

A lot of events, Francis Scott Fitzgerald portrayed in his novel "The Great Gatsby", are events he attended in his early life. The protagonist, Nick Carraway is a very educated and thoughtful Ivy League graduate from Minnesota who moved to New York like Fitzgerald.

Jay Gatsby also has similarities with Fitzgerald. Both idolized wealth und luxury and fell in love with a woman while serving for the country. Gatsby and Fitzgerald were driven by the love for a woman who was the only thing they wanted even though she led him down a couple times.

"Almost any perceptive reader will see that Fitzgerald, either consciously or unconsciously, brought his internal conflicts into his fiction. But this is not to say that his fiction does not also have a meaning entirely independent of his personal life."[11]

"The Great Gatsby" represents Fitzgerald's try to deal and confront himself with the Jazz Age.

---

[11] *The Great Gatsby*, Understanding, Dalton Gross & Maryjean Gross (1998)

5. Is the Great Gatsby easier to understand after reading Fitzgerald's biography?

It is very clear that you would understand the book without his biography. The whole book is conclusive and makes sense.

After you read his biography it is even easier to understand because you know what he wrote and you know why he wrote "The Great Gatsby" like he did. Reasons are easier to extrapolate and you can connect a lot of his elements used in his novel with aspects of his actual life. That makes it more interesting and contributes to the comprehension. Furthermore you can understand the feelings, Fitzgerald put in the novel and the thinking of the different characters. Most characters are endowed with vitality and they become very virtual after reading his biography. Because of his intertwining of his work with his life, his use of biographical elements contributes to a better understanding of „The Great Gatsby". Although a lot of major writers use biographical material in their fiction, does not mean that they will use created fiction for writing about their lives. One can see that Fitzgerald brought his own conflicts into the novel and to understand those conflicts, it helps to read his biography.

All in all "The Great Gatsby", written by Francis Scott Fitzgerald, is one of the greatest novels in

American history, which reveals a look into the
roaring twenties, celebrated by the wealthy people.

6. Literaturverzeichnis

- Philippe Lejeune, "Autobiographical Pact,"
  pg. 19
- *Afternoon of an Author*, ed. Arthur Mizener
  (New York: Scribners, 1958), p. 132.
- *The Notebooks of F. Scott Fitzgerald,* ed.
  Matthew J. Bruccoli (New York and
  London: Harcourt Brace
  Jovanovich/Bruccoli Clark, 1978), # 1072.
- "One Hundred False Starts," *Afternoon of
  an Author,* p. 132.
- Scrapbook, Princeton; the clipping is
  reproduced in the *Fitzgerald/Hemingway
  Annual* (1976), p. 108
- The Great Gatsby, Methuen Notes (Study
  Aids, 1978)
- *The Great Gatsby*, Understanding, Dalton
  Gross & Maryjean Gross (1998)
- Letter from Fitzgerald, Fitzgerald (97)
- http://gatsbyprojecttahs.wikispaces.com/Ga
  tsby+connection+to+Fitzgerald
- http://www.shmoop.com/great-
  gatsby/society-class-theme.html